Chester Creek Ravine

Chester
Creek
Ravine

Haiku

*To Gary &
Ramona,
in [illegible],
Bart Sutter*

Bart Sutter

ISBN: 978-1-935666-75-2

Library of Congress Cataloging-in-Publication Data

Sutter, Barton, 1949-
  [Poems. Selections]
  Chester Creek ravine : haiku / by Barton Sutter.
      pages ; cm
  ISBN 978-1-935666-75-2
  1. Haiku, American. I. Title.
  PS3569.U87A6 2015
  811'.54--dc23

                                    2015008403

Nodin Press, LLC
5114 Cedar Lake Road
Minneapolis, MN 55416

For

Lilo and Bettina

A stem of lupine
  Left on the sign
For the hiking trail.

Contents

Spring

Weeks away from blossoms,
 We stand and watch the water run
  Over the rocky bottom.

    ❀

 Spring at last? It has to be:
A pair of woolen mittens
  Stuck in a leafless tree.

    ❀

Ice about gone,
 The woods a room swept clean,
  The party coming on.

A soft and fragrant breeze
    Drifts along the ground. The earth itself
      Seems to whisper, "Please."

            ❧

    Thunder of the creek!
      With so much noise, who can hear
    The song sparrow speak?

            ❧

Now the green blades shove
    Past last year's ratty oak leaves
      Like abandoned gloves.

An ice arch rots
    Above the waterfall. Some things
We keep, some not.

          🌲

In April we're relieved
    To hear the bare trees fill with song.
      We can wait for leaves.

In sneakers and a stocking cap,
　　The pregnant girl throws a stick,
　　And there goes her black lab!

　　　　　　　　❧

　　Winter, slow to go,
　　Went north, then came back overnight.
　　Robins in the snow.

Who said April's cruel?
        Here's a pair of mallards
In a quiet pool.

❧

A great big fellow,
        Towing two puppies on leashes,
                Nods and says hello.

❧

        We barely dare believe,
Yet here's a branch of buds and there
        The littlest leaves.

Good to hear the robins talk,
    To stand and watch the water
      Curl around a rock.

❧

    Who wants to be responsible?
  Why not sit out all night? The glint
    Of a bum's pint bottle.

❧

The creek is in a rush,
    Tumbling headlong toward the lake,
      But not this hermit thrush.

Our beautiful friend
Is dying of cancer; the buds
Keep coming anyway.

Now I'm an old grump,
I feel a great affinity
With woodpecker stumps.

After days of rain,
    An opening in the sky.
    Gull cry.

❧

Now we come alive.
    Tufts of dormant grass
Sprout like clumps of chive.

❧

Buds, pastel and pale,
    Stipple the warming woods,
    A decorated veil.

The song of the robin
        You longed for last month—
Already monotonous.

It's enough to make you clap:
        Birds flit by with grass and twigs;
        A man removes his cap.

An older fellow,
    Breathing hard, stops to caress
      The pussy willow.

❦

A pair of mallards,
    An old married couple,
Waddle up the trail.

❦

Now the world is new:
    Instead of frost this morning,
      We get sparkling dew.

His fingers numb,
    And stung by sleet, the old man stops
To sniff the wild plum.

Spring takes the land:
    A girl with jacket round her waist,
        Both gloves in one hand.

I can't stay sad
    While walking through perfume
    Of Balm of Gilead.

                ❀

The crow above the creek
    Keeps cursing flowing water
    In a fit of pique.

Here in the ravine,
    I turn willowy and green. The dog
        Runs down to lap the stream.

           ❧

A natural composition:
    Withered mountain ash berries,
  Fresh flowers of the plum.

           ❧

On the muddy trail,
    A sudden blossom shower,
      Petals white and frail.

Branches, even logs,
Wash past in fast water.
"Hey!" I call the dog.

❧

How the dog's tail wags!
I bring home wildflowers
And windblown plastic bags.

❧

Now it's spring, besides
Plum blossoms, we must also
Greet the flies.

High above the trees,
　　Flapping, honking urgently,
A late flock of geese.

Summer

They come as pleasant shocks,
    The first wild strawberries,
White and purple phlox.

         ❀

    Face-deep in pollen,
        A bumblebee has landed
On a big fat dandelion.

         ❀

The ferns burst forth.
    Odd to find jungle
        So far north.

In streamside scenery,
    The best part is invisible:
        Birdsong in the greenery.

❧

Oh, a raindrop!
    Reminding me I'm fifty-nine,
With a bald spot.

❧

When she flutters by,
It snows although it's summer—
    Cabbage butterfly.

Breathing hard, we stall.
    Crows, too, have stopped to rest
      Beside the waterfall.

       Drenched with warm raindrops,
    I watch the foaming river
      That will not be stopped.

Warming on a rock
　　After a long night of rain,
　　　　The year's first mourning cloak.

　　🌺

　　What's a little arthritis
As long as you can walk the trail
　　And still see wild iris?

At last let out of school,
    The boy with thick-lensed glasses
        Stands knee-deep in the pool.

Although it's just June 1,
    In dandelions gone to seed,
Autumn has begun.

Cottontail, I see you
Enter a hole in the woods.
    I would go there, too.

To my right, a log rots;
    To my left, a cloud of pale
        Blue forget-me-nots.

❦

I thought I was alone,
    But I hear women's voices,
Water over stone.

❦

That rain was so rude
    Even the wren
        Sounds sort of subdued.

I was just daydreaming
Till a runner galloped past,
   Her blonde hair streaming.

They go round the bend,
   A bucket stretched between them,
   My neighborhood friends.

We hear the water rush
    As we examine buttercups,
    Indian paintbrush.

He watches a mink
Slink along the bank, then vanish
    When he blinks.

Chin-deep in clover,
    The chipmunk quits chewing
    To look me over.

    ❧

    Here on the cliff-top,
Talking to his radio,
    A bewildered cop.

    ❧

There comes a pause
    Amid the violence, huge logs
Perched above the falls.

The bee would like to marry
    The simple white wild rose
      Of the thimbleberry.

    Way back in there,
Tiny songsters. Doesn't it sound like
    They're sewing the air?

Clothes hung up to dry.
    Nobody nearby. This must be
    A hobo's laundry day.

    In this hungry world
Are many dangers, and I'm one,
    According to this red squirrel.

Waiting for the crash
    Of civilization, I still
    Bend to pick up trash.

The cuckoo clucks
    From deep green shade. Shy people,
        Too, get sort of stuck.

All night, thunder talks.
    By morning, many petals
Lie scattered on the rocks.

Carrying his kill,
The goshawk cut across the path.
I hear wing beats still.

Dan, the volunteer,
    Repairs the path with mud. He,
Too, is thoroughly smeared.

I'm stopped in my tracks
    By the little girl who smiles
        From her mom's backpack.

Somebody cares
    Enough to make a sign:
        "Hornets nest on stairs."

        ❀

A robin hurries past.
    A few yellow willow leaves
        Have fallen in the path.

        ❀

How should I handle
These surprises on the trail?
Here is one pink sandal.

Wood smoke on the breeze.
The heavy-headed grasses
Bow as summer passes.

.

Fall

Now that summer's done,
    The crabapples have deepened
        From dark red to plum.

✿

        College girls in shorts
    Jog past. Pretty, tan, and tough,
        They gasp for breath and snort.

✿

Bright leaves bedeck the forest floor,
    So now we see the rushing stream
We only heard before.

Water flies right off the cliff.
　　Too late to say,
　　　　"Wait now. What if … "

❀

There! See how it flits
Among the green and golden leaves?
　　Golden-crowned kinglet.

❀

Bright sun, a light breeze.
　　Suddenly, across the creek,
　　　　I hear someone sneeze.

No one scattered these
Golden popple leaves, yet we
Proceed like royalty.

A pair of red squirrels playing tag.
"Are you prepared for ten below?"
Someone has to nag!

I've been booze-free for years.
    Down the foaming rapids
        The water pours like beer.

Here they come, singing,
Before the leaves have fallen,
        The small pine siskins.

A girl in sweats, who jogs,
    A woman with her coffee mug,
        An old man and his dog.

❀

    Dying leaves and sunlight blend.
The dog and I both stop to sniff,
        Mystified by wind.

❀

    A crumpled blue beer can
        Beside the waterfall.
           Man, oh, man.

The willow tree with half a trunk
Survives ... at least so far.
The nation still at war.

❀

Who's afraid to die
When steps turn crisp with leaves,
A golden stairway to the sky?

❀

Wind-whipped clouds above.
Down here, the ferns have turned.
Glad I've got my gloves.

Here's where he was lost.
To the tree beside the cliff
Someone's tied a cross.

Dan, the volunteer,
Trims trees with his loppers.
A woodpecker is also here.

Here's a water bead
  On a tiny moccasin
    Of the jewelweed.

❧

Now, as she grows older,
  She often stops to lay a hand
On this mossy boulder.

❧

Here's a hollow birch.
  "Anybody home?"
    An empty church.

Catching evening light,
They cling, these last birch leaves,
Who don't believe in spring.

🌸

Deep in Chester Creek ravine—
Here, too, the scarlet splash
Of the mountain ash.

White-throated sparrows,
    With their pine-scented songs,
        Will be gone tomorrow.

Six months until we see new buds.
Water drips from naked twigs,
    Black leaves on black mud.

At this pretty view,
Fritz wrote his name on rock.
    He'll be gone soon, too.

🌳

A bad election
    Last night. Below the bridge
        At dawn: smashed pumpkins.

🌳

The wind gave the trees
    Such a thrashing I felt
        Sorry for the bees.

Holy cripes!
At the top of the ravine,
The yowl of bagpipes!

❧

Birds' nests in bare woods,
So much flotsam left behind
By last spring's flood.

❧

The evening primrose
Ignores its name and opens
As the sunrise glows.

The leaves all molder.
This lichen-spattered boulder
Melts more slowly.

Somebody's trousers
Hang from a branch, fifty feet
Above the creek.

Gather fallen oak
    Leaves to make a centerpiece.
Hear that raven croak?

    The big woodpecker
Flaps his wings and swerves. This path
    Is also full of curves.

From branches in the stream,
    Icicles begin to drip.
        Last summer was a dream.

Elegant, light gray,
   This wasp nest like a lantern
   Just might show the way.

Winter

Now their seeds are shed,
    Pale grasses wait
With clasped hands and bowed heads.

After a sleetstorm,
    The path becomes the one place
        Where you should not walk.

Cedars grow from rock
    And don't complain or brag.
        They let the water talk.

With soft snow falling,
　　We walk right through
　　　A charcoal drawing.

☙

　　What's this, a dead deer?
　An afghan filled with birch bark
　Left abandoned here.

Summer's truly gone.
  Creek ice forms overnight;
    Light snow falls at dawn.

The dog acts finicky
As she surveys first ice this year …
  Then crosses quickly, quickly!

I've got my share of woe;
  The mountain ash berries
    Carry loads of snow.

Out here in the cold,
The woodpeckers tap telegraph,
But we can't crack their code.

❧

That snowfall was a beaut.
No sound now but chickadees,
The creaking of my boots.

❧

Beside the creek, I squint
And wonder at the tail track
That snakes between paw prints.

What in tarnation?
To this tiny pine tree someone's tied
   A Christmas decoration.

I've burned up two weeks
   Cleaning house and offices.
Bright new snow on Chester Creek.

Sunlight floods the draw.
  A crow sings hallelujah
    Crudely: "Yah! Yah! Yah!"

    She's eager for the trail,
So far ahead already
    I only see her tail.

Out of banks and berms,
    The water seeps and freezes
White as milk or sperm.

❧

    I hear a red squirrel buzz,
The snowcrunch of my boots. Who knew
    How noisy summer was?

❧

Bare dogwood stands out,
    A natural calligraphy
        Written in red ink.

Everything shrunk tight.
   The sun hangs in the sky,
      An Inuit drum.

         ❧

   Goldfinches flock
To see the wicked winter through,
   To search for seeds and some sweet talk.

         ❧

The dog and I stand looking
   At a black hole in the ice.
      Sounds like something's cooking!

In colored coveralls,
   The climbers talk a long time
      Below the frozen falls.

      Four big birches grown
  Out of the same stump. Siblings
    Who stayed close to home.

This snowstorm stings like hail.
The dog still poops politely
In a boot print off the trail.

Winter's fierce and long,
But isn't that the chickadee's
Two-note mating song?

No need for speeches
　　About spring. Dogs gallop free,
　　　　Dragging their leashes.

　　　　✿

　　Jammed with ice and snow,
Chester Creek discovers
　　A different way to go.

　　　　✿

In this wintry Eden,
　　I hear someone singing.
　　　　My ancestors in Sweden.

Long after she has died,
   I'll still recall this little dog
      Prancing through the pines.

         ❧

   They laid these stones with skill,
But how'd they haul them down here
To hold back the hill?

         ❧

Water rumbles under
   Ice. Could that be where
      They store the thunder?

Weeks ago, creek ice froze.
    A pileated whacks a trunk.
    I hear axe blows.

       ❧

All night, snow fell,
    And still it falls. The dog and I
Both blink. Church bells.

Who cares about the cold?
After all this murk, bright light,
Shadows sharp and bold.

We like the look of mud.
Desperate for spring, we think
Raindrops might be buds.

Riding in a chestpack,
Babbling nonsense, the baby
Makes his mother laugh.

Thirty-one degrees.
The scarlet notes of a cardinal,
Sunlight through the trees.

Where have all the hikers gone?
The fire ring beside the stream
Filled with fallen leaves.

ACKNOWLEDGMENTS

I am grateful to the editors of the following publications in which some of these poems appeared: "Face-deep in pollen," "The bee would like to marry," and "The wind gave the trees," in *If Bees are Few*; "Now the world is new" in *Talking River Review;* "The cuckoo clucks" and "The ferns burst forth" in *Verse Wisconsin.*

Thanks to Cheryl Dannenbring, Dorothea Diver, Milan Kovacovic, Ilze Mueller, and Walt Prentice for their critical comments and encouragement. Startled appreciation to Jean Replinger for financial support. My gratitude to Norton Stillman and John Toren of Nodin Press for their careful work on this book, and to Cecilia Lieder for her artwork inspired by the ravines of Duluth. And thanks to two dogs, Sophie and Tayla, now dead, for their companionship in the ravine.